709·03

D1342027

Artists in Profile

POST-IMPRESSIONISTS

Linda Bolton

www.heinemann.co.uk/library
Visit our website to find out more information about **Heinemann Library** books.

To order:
 Phone 44 (0) 1865 888066
Send a fax to 44 (0) 1865 314091
 Visit the Heinemann Bookshop at www.heinemann.co.uk/library to browse our catalogue and order online.

First published in Great Britain by Heinemann Library, Halley Court, Jordan Hill, Oxford OX2 8EJ, a part of Harcourt Education. Heinemann is a registered trademark of Harcourt Education Ltd.

© Harcourt Education Ltd 2002
The moral right of the proprietor has been asserted.

Editorial: Jilly Attwood and ClaireThrop
Design: Jo Hinton-Malivoire and Tinstar Design Limited (www.tinstar.co.uk)
Picture Research: Catherine Bevan
Production: Lorraine Warner

Originated by Ambassador Litho Ltd
Printed and bound in China by South China Printing Company

ISBN 0 431 11641 5
06 05 04 03 02
10 9 8 7 6 5 4 3 2 1

British Library Cataloguing in Publication Data
Bolton, Linda
    Post–Impressionists. – (Artists in profile)
    709'.0346
A full catalogue record for this book is available from the British Library.

Acknowledgements
The publishers would like to thank the following for permission to reproduce photographs: AKG London p**46**, AKG London/Narodni Galerie Prag p**55**, AKG London/Private Collection, Paris p**53**; Art Institute of Chicago, IL, USA/Bridgeman Art Library p**47**; Baden, Stiftung "Langmatt", AKG London p**4**; Collection Mr & Mrs Donald S. Stralen/AKG London p**10**; Collection Oskar Reinhart, Winterthur/AKG London p**13**; Corbis/Francis G. Mayer p**51**; Galleria degli Uffizi, Florence/Erich Lessing/AKG London p**16**; Gift of Audrey Jones Beck/Museum of Fine Arts, Houston, Texas, USA/Bridgeman Art Library p**21**; Hermitage, St. Petersburg, Russia/Bridgeman Art Library p**37**; J.P. Zenobel/Musee Maurice Denis, St. Germain-en-Laye/Bridgeman Art Library p**44**, J.P. Zenobel/Rijksmuseum Vincent Van Gogh, Amsterdam, The Netherlands/Bridgeman Art Library p**29**; Kahnweiler Collection, Musee National d'Art Moderne, Paris/AKG London p**50**; Musee des Beaux-Arts Andre Malraux, Le Havre, France/Giraudon/Bridgeman Art Library p**22**; Musee d'Orsay, Paris, France/Erich Lessing/AKG London pp **8**, **17**, **25**, **31**, **39**, **40**, **49**, Musee d'Orsay, Paris/Lauros/Giraudon/Bridgeman Art Library p**5**, Musee d'Orsay/Bridgeman p**43**; Musee Matisse, Le Chateau-Cambresis/AKG London p**35**; National Gallery of Scotland, Edinburgh/Bridgeman Art Library p**26**; Nelson-Atkins Museum of Art, Kansas City/AKG London p**15**; Private Collection, France/Erich Lessing/AKG London p**48**; Private Collection/Bridgeman Art Library pp **11**, **23**; Rijksmuseum Vincent Van Gogh, Amsterdam, The Netherlands/Bridgeman Art Library p**32**; Roger Viollet pp **19**, **45**, Roger-Viollet, Paris/Musee Gustave Moreau, Paris, France/Bridgeman Art Library p**38**; San Francisco Museum of Modern Art/Bequest of Harriet Lane Levy p**6**.

The cover photograph shows *The Café Terrace* by Vincent van Gogh (1888). This image is reproduced with permission of B & U International.

Our thanks to Richard Stemp for his help in the preparation of this book.

Author dedication
For my daughter Anastasia with love.

Contents

Words appearing in the text in bold, **like this**, are explained in the glossary.

What is Post-Impressionism?

One of the main things to remember about Post-Impressionism is that rather than being a separate style in itself, it was actually a collection of different responses to Impressionism. The artists who we consider to be Post-Impressionists did not think of themselves as Post-Impressionists. The name was given to them in 1910 by the English artist and critic Roger Fry. He was keen to organize an exhibition of modern French art. 'What shall we call it – this new exhibition of modern French painting?' 'Expressionism', was one term he came up with, but decided not to use. Fry thought that Impressionist art was superficial – that it was full of charm, but not serious. He did admire the work of Manet, however, and his final exhibition title, 'Manet and the Post-Impressionists', deliberately excludes the work of the Impressionists.

▐▌ *Still Life,* by Paul Cézanne (1890)
Cézanne frequently painted still-lifes to examine the structure of immobile objects. He used a palette knife to lay on touches of paint, and to create a sense of volume by using complimentary colours, like red and green, next to each other.

The exhibition opened in London on 8 November 1910. It introduced the British public to the work of Manet, Cézanne, Gauguin, van Gogh, Seurat and several others. These artists had all been associated with the Impressionists, and been influenced by the bright, light colours that the Impressionists were using, but each of them developed individual and new ways of making paintings – new approaches to colour, **perspective** and subject.

The emphasis of Fry's exhibition was on Gauguin, van Gogh and Cézanne, and the impact this exhibition had on the British viewers who visited it was immense. The bright, strong colours and bold **composition** were a revelation to the exhibition visitors.

Starry Night over the Rhône, by Vincent van Gogh (1888)
Van Gogh painted this scene at night by the light of a gas jet. He wrote about it to his brother Theo, describing the greenish–blue of the sky, the royal blue of the water and the blue and violet of the town, lit by gas light. In the foreground are two lovers, a symbol of love and hope.

5

Fauvism

Fauvism was the term coined by the French art critic Louis Vauxcelles on viewing the 1905 **Salon d'Automne** exhibition in Paris. There he saw the bright, wild-looking paintings of Matisse, Derain, Vlaminck, Marquet, Manguin, Rouault and others, and described them as *fauves* or wild beasts.

The Fauves were not a definite, coherent group, but Matisse was considered a leader of sorts. The Fauves themselves had been strongly influenced by the great Post-Impressionists, Cézanne, Seurat, van Gogh and Gauguin, whose work they had seen in Paris in the early 1900s. They admired the way the painters had used strong, bright colours, and the way people, objects and landscapes were often flattened and simplified.

The Girl with Green Eyes, by Henri Matisse (1908)
This work shows the Fauve use of bold, flat colour and simplified form. The woman's features are given a simple linear treatment, and the objects in the background have a distinctively bright and modern appearance.

Symbolism

Symbolism was a literary as well as an artistic movement. Symbolist artists were against making things look real, and wanted instead a more idealized, dreamlike or imaginary approach to art. There are two distinct tendencies in Symbolism. The first, championed by artists like Gauguin, Sérusier, Denis and Bernard, dates from Gauguin's second visit to Pont-Aven (an artist's community in Brittany, northern France) in 1888. The style involved simplifying figures and objects, painting them as flat shapes and using a bold outline to enclose each area of colour.

The second tendency in Symbolism looked back to a mythical, dreamlike past. These artists, such as Puvis de Chavannes, Redon and Moreau, were dreamers who lived in their imagination, in a world of mystery and enchantment. They were influenced by a group of English painters called the Pre-Raphaelites, who often painted scenes from the tales of King Arthur and his knights. They showed their work at the annual exhibition mysteriously named the **Salon** de la Rose+Croix (The Exhibition of the Rose and Cross) organized in Paris from 1892 to 1897 by the extraordinary self-styled magician Josephin Péladan.

Nabis

A splinter group was formed from this second set of Symbolist artists, which took the name '**Nabis**' which is Hebrew for prophets. This was a group of students who had come together at the end of 1888 in Paris to form a secret brotherhood. They had met at art school – the Académie Julian, Paris – and showed their work together from 1891 to 1899. They believed in giving a more personal response to the subject they were painting rather than simply copying it in a realistic way.

The group existed due to the influence of Paul Sérusier. He had produced a painting called *The Talisman* under the direct influence of Paul Gauguin in Pont-Aven. He had used the new 'synthetism' approach that focused on flat areas of highly contrasting colours. When he returned to Paris he expressed Gauguin's views to his contemporaries and the group became known as the Nabis.

In terms of its importance in the history of art, Symbolism contributed as much as Impressionism to the development of **abstract** art. The movement also produced a number of imaginative paintings that prefigured the dream imagery of the 20th-century **Surrealists**.

Neo-Impressionism

One of the several different styles that was adopted by artists at this time, notably Georges Seurat and Paul Signac, was **Pointillism**, otherwise known as Neo-Impressionism. The artists themselves called it Divisionism and it was based on a scientific theory of optical mixing described by Ogden Rood in his 1879 book *Modern Chromatics*. The theory argued that different colours placed side by side in dots or very small brush strokes merge together when viewed from a distance, resulting in the viewer seeing one new colour. Seurat's painting *A Sunday Afternoon on the Island of La Grande Jatte* was the first real example of Divisionism.

The Talisman, by Paul Sérusier (1888)
Painted on the lid of a cigar box by Sérusier, under the direction of Gauguin, this small landscape was called The Talisman *or* Lucky Charm *as it served to show how a painting should be conceived: in strong, bright colour and form.*

Paris

Most of the artists that we now call Post-Impressionists worked mainly in Paris, although many were from other countries. Paris was considered to be the art capital of the world at that time. There was an intense concentration of artistic activity and art dealers, and the École des Beaux-Arts and Académie Julian were key schools where many artists were taught.

Key exhibitions that helped make these artists known included the official **Salon**, the **Salon des Refusés**, **Salon des Indépendants**, **Salon d'Automne**, **Les Vingt** (based in Belgium), the annual **Venice Biennale** and the Société des Artistes Indépendants, set up by Georges Seurat and Paul Signac.

The Salon

The Salon was the official art exhibition in Paris and, until 1863, had maintained firm control over which artists could display their work and also the kind of work that could be exhibited. Creative artists, including the Impressionists, protested to such an extent that in 1863, the Emperor, Napoleon III, ordered a special exhibition to be set up, called the Salon des Refusés, for those artists who were rejected from the Salon. This was a real breakthrough for artists who wanted to develop beyond the traditional techniques and subject matter. Cézanne was one of the artists who showed paintings there. Artists were now free to paint as they wished, secure in the knowledge that they would not face constant rejection from exhibitions if their art did not match the traditionally favoured styles.

Many of the artists were also helped considerably by the main art dealers in Paris. These included the galleries of Ambroise Vollard and Paul Durand-Ruel as well as the Bernheim-Jeune Gallery. Other patrons of Post-Impressionist art included Gertrude Stein, whose family bought many pieces of work from artists such as Matisse.

The effect of war

The Franco-Prussian War of 1870–71 between France and Prussia resulted in a crushing defeat for France. While most of the Post-Impressionists were too young to have fought, Puvis de Chavannes and Redon both served in the war. Many artists were more affected by both World Wars, especially World War I (1914–18) when many, including Derain, were drafted to fight.

Pierre Bonnard 1867–1947

- Born on 3 October 1867 in the Paris suburb of Fontenay-aux-Roses.
- Died on 23 January 1947 at Le Cannet, in the South of France.

Key works
Dining Room in Country, 1913
The Window, 1925
Dining Room on the Garden, 1934–35

Pierre Bonnard was born on 3 October 1867 in the Paris suburb of Fontenay-aux-Roses. He was the second of three children born to François, a civil servant at the Ministry of War and his wife Elizabeth Mertzdorff. Much of his childhood was spent in the countryside where his family owned a house in a large park, and from an early age he developed a love of animals and the country.

Self-portrait, by Pierre Bonnard (1945)
Painted in his house in the South of France three years before his own death, and three years after the death of his lifetime companion Marthe, the ageing painter presents an image of loneliness.

After leaving high school in 1885 Bonnard enrolled in the law faculty to please his father, and at the same time declared that he wanted to devote his free time to the serious study of painting. In 1887 he enrolled at the Académie Julian where he met Denis, Sérusier, Ibels and Ranson who together formed the group known as the **Nabis**. In 1888 he gained his law degree and worked part-time in a record office. He was also admitted to the École des Beaux-Arts.

In 1889 he won first prize for a poster design for the France-Champagne company. The 100-franc prize encouraged him to continue as an artist and won the respect of his father, but the same year he was called up to do his compulsory **military service**.

On his return to Paris in 1890 Bonnard shared a studio with Denis and Vuillard, and in 1891 he exhibited at the **Salon des Indépendants**. He also showed in the Impressionist and **Symbolist** Painters exhibitions. The latter provided the first group showing of the Nabis.

Bonnard was greatly influenced by Japanese prints, having seen an exhibition of Japanese art at the École des Beaux-Arts in 1890. He admired the simplicity and use of colour within these works and incorporated it into his own work. He was described by one critic in 1892 as 'the most Japanese of all French painters'.

Like other Nabis artists, Bonnard made his living, from 1891 to 1905, as a decorator, graphic artist and designer. He made screens, posters, **lithographs**, theatre designs and illustrations.

In 1893 he met Marie Boursin, known as Marthe, who became his model and lifelong companion, and he had his first solo exhibition in 1896 at Paul Durand-Ruel's gallery. While the art critic Gustave Geffroy praised it, the artist Camille Pissarro said: 'One more Symbolist who is a total failure.' Pissarro also claimed that Puvis de Chavannes, Degas, Renoir and Monet all found the exhibition hideous. However, Pissarro's opinion later changed, and Redon and Monet also admired Bonnard. Indeed, years later Bonnard helped to carry the coffin at Monet's funeral.

The art dealer Ambroise Vollard had been buying prints from Bonnard for some time, but in 1900 the firm Bernheim-Jeune became Bonnard's art dealer. From 1905 he could afford to travel and visited Spain, Belgium and Holland. From 1910 he divided his time between Paris and the South of France and bought a country house in Normandy in 1912. World War I meant that he had to stop travelling and settle down, eventually buying a house at Le Cannet in the South of France.

From the 1920s Bonnard lived a quiet existence as a painter with occasional commissions as an illustrator. In 1923 he was awarded third prize in the **Carnegie International** Exhibition, Pittsburgh, and there was a **retrospective** of his art the following year. In 1925 he married Marthe. She was the woman he painted repeatedly in the bath, at the breakfast table, robing and disrobing in different rooms. It is the record of these small, intimate moments that gave him and Vuillard the title '**Intimists**'.

Marthe died in 1942 and Bonnard was cared for by his niece until his death at Le Cannet in January 1947.

▌▌ *Woman in a Check Dress*, by Pierre Bonnard (1891)
This joining of image and pattern shows the sort of decorative work which made Bonnard popular as a graphic artist and in demand as a designer of posters and screen.

Paul Cézanne 1839–1906

- Born on 19 January 1839 in Aix-en-Provence in the South of France.
- Died on 22 October 1906 in Aix-en-Provence, France.

Key works

Mont Sainte-Victoire, c. 1887
Apples and Oranges, c. 1899
Man with Crossed Arms, c. 1899

Paul Cézanne was born on 19 January 1839 in Aix-en-Provence in the South of France. His father, Louis-Auguste Cézanne, was a hatter. His mother, Anne Elizabeth Honorine Aubert, was a housewife. Cézanne had a younger sister, Marie, who was born in 1842. Cézanne and his sister were **illegitimate**. However, in 1844 his parents married and the children were **legitimized**.

Cézanne's father became a banker, and the family were financially comfortable. After attending the local school Cézanne became a boarder at the Collége Bourbon where he was an excellent student and won a prize for painting. At the College he met the writer, Emile Zola, and they remained close friends until 1886.

In 1857 Cézanne registered at a free drawing school but following his father's wishes he enrolled in law school in Aix in December 1859. Cézanne had little interest in the subject and continued to paint while studying. His one desire was to move to Paris where his childhood friend Zola was living and learn to paint. Zola encouraged him to move, and eventually, in the face of parental opposition, Cézanne left Aix for Paris in April 1861. Failing to secure a place at the École des Beaux-Arts he returned to Aix for a spell and worked in his father's bank, but returned once more to Paris in early November. In 1863 he exhibited at the notorious **Salon des Refusés**, and the following year was rejected by the **Salon**, the first of many rejections through 1864 to 1869.

In 1870 he avoided the call-up for **military service** at the outbreak of the Franco-Prussian War, and lived at L'Estaque, the coastal region of Provence in the South of France, with Hortense Fiquet, his model. They had met the year before, and she bore him a son two years later. In January 1871 he was declared a draft dodger (someone who avoided military service), and returned to Paris only when the fighting was over.

■■■ *Self-portrait*, by Paul Cézanne (c. 1879–82)
Cézanne in his early forties presents a melancholic self-portrait. Although admired by a small group of younger artists, including Gauguin, Cézanne wondered, in some desperation, if his work would ever find wider recognition.

The year 1873 was spent in Auvers-sur-Oise where Cézanne walked daily to Pontoise to see the Impressionist painter, Camille Pissarro, who was a great influence on him. He was introduced to Dr Gachet, collector of Impressionist paintings. In 1874 the first Impressionist exhibition was staged, and Pissarro insisted that Cézanne be allowed to exhibit three paintings.

During the years 1875 to 1886 Cézanne lived in a variety of places including Aix, L'Estaque, Gardanne, Marseilles, Pointoise and Paris. However, he felt most at home in Provence and was unwilling to abandon it for Paris. He did not show at the second Impressionist exhibition but exhibited sixteen works at the third. They were not well received and Cézanne despaired that he would ever achieve the recognition he felt he deserved. The public did not like his work but other artists began to show an interest. Gauguin, for example, wrote to his wife in December 1885 begging her not to sell his two Cézannes and telling her that 'they are rare ... and one day they'll be quite valuable'.

In March 1886 Zola published L'Oeuvre (The Work), a novel about a hapless artist who loses his way and finds no success in the art world. Cézanne saw this as a reference to himself, was deeply hurt and broke off all contact with his childhood friend. On 28 April 1886 Cézanne married Hortense. Later that year his father died leaving him a substantial legacy. Cézanne was now able to work freely, liberated from money worries. In 1890 he was invited to exhibit in Brussels and took a holiday with his family in Switzerland. The following year he became a devout Catholic. He had been born a Catholic, but had not dedicated himself to religion as he did now.

In 1894 Cézanne visited Monet in Giverny. Monet was working almost solely in the garden he had created there, painting his water lilies at all times of day, light, weather and season. Cézanne took this idea as inspiration for his series of paintings based on Mont Sainte-Victoire in the South of France. He repeatedly painted the mountain, first seen as a view from the house bought by his brother-in-law in 1891. He did this in order to try to understand the structure of the landscape, rather than to capture the changing light as Monet was doing.

The year 1895 saw Cézanne's first one-man show at the art dealer Ambroise Vollard's gallery in Paris. He helped to establish Cézanne's fame, even buying all the work Cézanne had in his studio during 1897. In his mid fifties Cézanne found himself attracting a circle of admiring artists who wrote to him and made the pilgrimage to Aix to visit him. Despite this, Cézanne remained isolated with very few friends: people often complained of his mood swings and bad temper.

After the death of his mother in 1897 Cézanne sold the family home at Jas de Bouffan. He rented an apartment in Aix and planned the building of a new studio overlooking Aix. Ten of Cézanne's paintings were exhibited at the **Salon d'Automne** in Paris in 1906. On 15 October 1906 Cézanne collapsed while painting outside, dying a week later on 22 October from pneumonia. Exhibitions of his work in 1907 proved very influential on a body of younger artists, such as Matisse, Picasso and Braque.

The Mountain Sainte-Victoire, by Paul Cézanne (1902–06)
Cézanne repeatedly painted this mountain in his native Aix-en-Provence. He used it as a means of understanding the structure of landscape itself, constructing the image as a series of multi-faceted shapes.

Maurice Denis 1870–1943

- Born on 25 November 1870 at Granville, France.
- Died on 13 November 1943 in Paris.

Key works
Catholic Mystery, 1890
April, 1892, 1892
The Encounter, 1892

Self-portrait, by Maurice Denis (1916)
This self-portrait was painted during World War I, when Denis was 46, and at a time when his work had become entirely religious.

Maurice Denis was born at Granville on 25 November 1870. From 1881 to 1887 he studied at the famous Parisian school, the Lycée Condorcet, where the artists Édouard Vuillard and Paul Sérusier were also pupils. In 1887 he enrolled at the Académie Julian and he became a founder member of the group who called themselves **Nabis**.

In 1890 Denis wrote in the review *Art et Critique* a definition of painting that was to become famous: 'Remember that a painting – before being a war horse, a naked woman or some anecdote – is essentially a surface plane covered with colour arranged in a certain order.'

Denis showed with the Nabis in the **Salon des Indépendants** of 1891 and the Barc de Boutteville gallery, and the following year in Belgium. In 1893 he married the artist Marthe Meurier, and in 1895 made his first trip to Italy with Sérusier. He was profoundly influenced by the religious **frescoes** of the **Renaissance** artists, Giotto, Fra Angelico and Piero della Francesca, which he saw there. In 1899 the art dealer Ambroise Vollard showed his series of coloured **lithographs** entitled *Amour*.

In 1903 Denis travelled with Sérusier to Beuron, a German Benedictine monastery and centre for religious art. Here he made 216 wood engravings for the magazine *The Imitation of Jesus Christ* and decorated the chapel of Sacré-Coeur at Vésinet. In 1904 he showed his Italian studies in his first solo exhibition at the Druet Gallery and had his second solo exhibition at the Bernheim-Jeune Gallery in Paris in 1907.

Fellow Nabi artist Paul Ranson set up the Académie Ranson in Venice, Italy in 1908. That same year Denis went to Venice to visit Ranson. Ranson's death the following year meant that his wife took over as director and Denis was among those artist friends who helped by teaching classes.

Denis bought the priory at Saint-Germain-en-Laye in 1913, and from this point onwards his work, having been concerned largely with the spiritual, became exclusively religious. In 1919 he founded the Ateliers d'Art Sacré (Studios of Sacred Art) in Paris in an attempt to teach religious art.

In 1922 Denis married Elizabeth Graterolle. He continued to travel widely and became a member of the Académie des Beaux-Arts in 1932. He published several books, mainly on theories of art, such as *The History of Religious Art*, and then in 1942, *Sérusier, His Life and Art*. On 13 November 1943 he was killed in Paris, in a road accident on the Boulevard Saint-Michel.

Homage to Cézanne, by Maurice Denis (1900)
The very title of the work explains the veneration in which a younger group of artists, including Denis, held Cézanne. A number of painters are shown grouped around a Cézanne still-life. Its display on an easel in the centre of the painting invites us to join the group and admire it with them.

André Derain 1880–1954

- Born in Chatou near Paris, France on 17 June 1880.
- Died in Garches, Seine-et-Oise, on 8 September 1954.

Key works

Houses of Parliament at Night, 1905–06
The Pool of London, 1906
Still life, 1921–22

André Derain was born in Chatou near Paris on 17 June 1880, the son of a well-to-do pastry-chef and town councillor. At the age of fifteen Derain was given painting lessons with the two sons of a local landscape painter called Jacomin. At school Derain did well in art and science, graduating not only with the prize in natural science but also winning the drawing prize. Derain's parents considered that painting might be fine as a hobby for their son but decided that engineering would be a safer choice as a profession, and enrolled him at an engineering college in Paris. This college was close to the École des Beaux-Arts as well as the various free art academies. It was also not far from the Louvre Museum, and Derain began to spend time painting riverscapes and looking at paintings in the Louvre. It was here that he met an artist named Linaret who introduced him to his friends who were studying under Gustave Moreau at the École des Beaux-Arts. These included Georges Rouault and Henri Matisse. Derain was immediately interested in the work of Matisse, especially in his use of colour.

Derain was, like many young painters, influenced by the work of Cézanne, but in 1901 he saw the first big exhibition of the paintings of Vincent van Gogh on show at the Bernheim-Jeune Gallery in Paris. It made a huge impact on him. At the van Gogh exhibition Matisse introduced Derain to the artist Maurice de Vlaminck, although the two had already met by chance on a train between Paris and Chatou, and this led to the two young men sharing a studio for a while. The two painted together in a dining room of a derelict restaurant called 'La Baraque' on an island in the Seine, near Chatou, where they lived a **bohemian** lifestyle. Derain was supported financially by his parents while Vlaminck was married with a family. The two men greatly admired each other and were described by Maurice Denis as 'the geniuses from the suburbs'.

■ *This photograph shows Derain in middle age. In contrast to the popular image of the artist, Derain is shown in conservative dress and with serious expression.*

Derain and Vlaminck began to paint with pure, bright colour, but their time of working together was interrupted by Derain's compulsory **military service**. However, the two men wrote to each other, and this lengthy correspondence documents their ideas on and responses to art. Derain realized it would not be possible to paint seriously while serving. He read widely, painted intermittently, and hoped to write a novel, as Vlaminck had done, to supplement his meagre wages from the army.

In September 1904 he left the army and returned to Chatou to paint with Vlaminck and Matisse, returning frequently to the Louvre where he made drawings of **Renaissance** and **Baroque** works as well as Egyptian sculpture. In February 1905 Matisse introduced Derain to the art dealer Ambroise Vollard, who bought everything he saw on the walls of Derain's studio. On the strength of this, Matisse persuaded Derain's parents to increase their son's allowance.

Derain exhibited four pictures at the **Salon des Indépendants**. In the summer, Derain joined Matisse at Collioure in the South of France, and later that year took part in the famous exhibition at the **Salon d'Automne**, where the participating artists were described as 'fauves' or 'wild animals' on account of their strong use of colour and application of paint. Derain's portrait of Matisse and painting of the Pool of London both show this bright, deliberately non-**naturalistic** use of colour. Vollard, very impressed with the series of paintings Monet had made of the Thames, sent Derain to paint in London in 1905.

When Derain returned from London in 1906 he met Picasso while painting at L'Estaque. The following year he signed with Picasso's art dealer, Daniel-Henri Kahnweiler. Financially secure, Derain married Alice Géry, an ex-model and mistress of Picasso, and went to live in Montmartre.

Derain was also greatly influenced by African art. Around 1908 he experimented with the **Cubist** theories of Picasso and Braque and painted with Picasso in Spain and the South of France. In 1911 he abandoned Cubism for his so-called 'Gothic Period' in which he was heavily influenced by the early French and Italian **primitives**, many of whose works he had copied in the Louvre.

During World War I, he served in Champagne, on the Somme and at Verdun. He had his first one-man show in 1916 and subsequently worked on the decors for Diaghilev's Ballets Russes. He was a versatile artist and worked as a painter, sculptor, potter, designer and illustrator. He was not able to leave the army until 1919 but then began to move in artistic circles in Paris.

From the 1920s onwards Derain made many long visits to Italy and the South of France. He won the **Carnegie Prize** in 1928. He became more of an isolated figure during the 1930s and bought a house at Chambourcy for his family, while also keeping a home in Paris because it was easier to find models in the city.

Derain lived in Paris for most of World War II and remained relatively untouched by the **Nazis**. He could not be described as degenerate (people and art that fell outside the Nazis' narrow vision) like many of the **Expressionist** artists of the time. He was in fact officially invited to visit Germany and accepted in 1942. This led to many people avoiding him, believing he was a collaborator with the Nazis.

Relations with his wife by this time were bad, though she did agree to adopt an **illegitimate** child of his. After an illness that left him only partially sighted, they separated. Derain died in Garches, Seine-et-Oise, on 8 September 1954, as a result of complications following a car crash.

▚ *The Turning Road, L'Estaque,* by André Derain (1906)
The dramatic composition and use of colour typifies the fauve use of bold flat colour and daring composition. Trees appear to swerve and perspective is deliberately skewed.

Raoul Dufy 1877–1953

- Born 3 June 1877 in Le Havre, France.
- Died 23 March 1953 at Forcalquier, France.

Key works

Portrait of Suzanne Dufy, the Artist's Sister, 1904
Poppyfield at Lourdes, c. 1908

Raoul Dufy was born on 3 June 1877 in the northern French sea port of Le Havre. He was the second son of Léon Marius, an accountant for a small metals firm, and Marie-Eugénie Ida. Music was a big part of family life and two of Dufy's brothers went on to become musicians. From the age of fourteen, due to the family's financial problems, Dufy had to leave school and work as a bookkeeper. However, he still attended evening classes at the École des Beaux-Arts in Paris, where he met the artist Georges Braque.

Self-portrait, by Raoul Dufy (c. 1945)
Dufy's early work most resembled Impressionism, but after meeting Matisse in 1905 he converted to Fauvism.

In 1899 Dufy went to Paris to continue his studies. In 1903 he showed his work at the **Salon des Indépendants** for the first time. His work at this point was heavily influenced by the Impressionists, and also van Gogh, but in 1905 he met Matisse and was bowled over by his painting *Luxe, Calme et Volupté*. He admired Matisse's technique and use of colour. He changed his own style and joined the **Fauves**, but his fauvism was more restrained and decorative than that of Derain or Vlaminck.

In 1908 Dufy stayed with Braque in L'Estaque where both were working very much under the influence of Cézanne. **Retrospective** exhibitions had been staged by Cézanne's former dealer, Ambroise Vollard, and were proving popular with younger artists. The monochrome (single-colour) **Cubist** style that Dufy was experimenting with at this time was abandoned in 1909 when he met the fashion designer Paul Poiret. This meeting led to Dufy getting work as a textile designer. In 1912 he worked for a silk manufacturer, designing textiles for curtains and sofa covers, as well as silk scarves depicting elegant and fashionable scenes of casinos, racetracks and regattas.

In 1913 Dufy moved to Hyères in the South of France, and from 1920 to 1923 travelled widely in Italy. In 1925 he went to Morocco with Poiret and later that year showed the fourteen tapestries he made for Poiret at the International Exhibition of Decorative Arts. In 1930 he won the **Carnegie Prize** and from 1936 designed the decor for several venues in Paris: the Pavilion of Electricity, the monkey house in the Botanic Gardens and the theatre in the Palais de Chaillot. World War II saw him in the South of France in the fashionable world he so often depicted in his art.

At the age of 73 Dufy travelled to the USA for an operation on his hands, which had been affected by arthritis since 1837. In 1952 he won the International Grand Prix for painting at the **Venice Biennale** and also moved to Forcalquier because of its warmer climate. He died there the following year at the age of 76.

The Regatta at Cowes, by Raoul Dufy (1934)
This work is a perfect example of Dufy's bright, exuberant paintings with their holiday feel. His paintings of races and regattas where bunting and flags fly gaily in the breeze create a festive and joyful mood.

Paul Gauguin 1848–1903

- Born on 7 June 1848 in Paris, France.
- Died on 8 May 1903 in prison on the Marquesas islands.

Key works

The Vision after the Sermon (Jacob Wrestling with the Angel), 1888
In the Vanilla Grove, Man and Horse, 1891
A Farm in Brittany, 1894

Paul Gauguin was born in Paris in June 1848. The following year Gauguin's family set sail for Lima, Peru, where Gauguin's mother had family. His father, a political journalist, intended to start a newspaper there but collapsed and died on the ship. Gauguin's early years were spent in Peru with his mother and sister. On the death of his grandfather in 1855 the family returned to Orléans in France to claim their inheritance. Gauguin remembered Peru as a lost, golden world, an exotic and faraway place that he longed to return to. In 1865 an opportunity arose that allowed him to travel. He completed his compulsory **military service** in the French navy, when he sailed to South America from 1865 to 1867.

In 1867 Gauguin's mother died, and a family friend, Gustave Arosa, became his guardian. Arosa was a patron and collector of avant-garde works that provided Gauguin with his first introduction to the world of art. Arosa also found him work as a stockbroker, buying and selling shares, in Paris from 1871.

In the summer of 1873 Gauguin was encouraged to paint by Arosa's daughter Marguerite. Although he had no formal training, his early works are remarkably accomplished. In 1873 he married a Danish woman named Mette Sophie Gad, and in 1874 their son Emile was born. In 1876 his painting *Landscape at Viroflay* was accepted by the **Salon** and he started to collect Impressionist paintings. Between 1879 and 1882 he exhibited with the Impressionists and showed nineteen paintings in the last Impressionist exhibition.

By 1883 Gauguin had given up his job in the banking firm to devote himself to painting. Finding himself unable to make a living as a painter in Paris he moved with his family to Rouen where the cost of living was lower and where the artist Camille Pissarro, whom Gauguin had met through Arosa, was working. Still unable to make ends meet, Gauguin and his family moved to Copenhagen in 1885 to live with Mette's family. By now Gauguin and Mette were on very bad terms. In desperation he tried to sell tarpaulins (waterproof protective coverings) in an attempt to provide for his family.

Finally Gauguin decided to try to seek work back in France and taking his son Clovis, he returned to Paris in June 1886. In desperate poverty he put Clovis in boarding school, and free of family responsibilities, he made his way to Pont-Aven, Brittany, where he remained for several months.

Brittany in northern France was still at this time a primitive region and this appealed to Gauguin, who liked to describe himself as 'a primitive savage'. The peasants still wore traditional costume and had a simple way of life. He painted them at work and in prayer in a deliberately **primitive**, naïve style where traditional **perspective** was replaced with a more vertical format, as seen in Japanese prints.

Self-portrait, by Paul Gauguin (c. 1896)
The artist has shown himself in profile, something he frequently did, to present a dramatic viewpoint. Many of his self-portraits show him as a suffering often Christ-like figure.

At the end of 1886 Gauguin severed his friendship with Pissarro and with the Impressionist style of painting. He saw much of Degas and met van Gogh. In April 1887 he set off for Panama 'to live like a savage', but fell ill while in Martinique and had to work his passage back to Marseilles.

In 1888 he returned to Pont-Aven where he gathered around him a group of young and admiring artists including Emile Bernard. He and Bernard developed a style of art known as Synthetism in which literature and music fused with painting.

He became a more confident painter through the support of Theo van Gogh, brother of the artist, Vincent. Later that year, attracted by the invitation of free board and lodging, Gauguin joined Vincent van Gogh in Arles. The relationship was not an easy one and ended with van Gogh's self-mutilation.

■ *The Vision after the Sermon (Jacob Wrestling with the Angel),* by Paul Gauguin (1888)
One of the artist's most powerful paintings, this image shows Breton women in their traditional dress imagining the theme of the sermon they have just heard: the biblical story of Jacob and the angel, pictured in the upper right of the canvas.

Emile Bernard 1868–1941

Emile Bernard was born in Lille on 28 April 1868, son of a cloth merchant. In 1884 he enrolled as a student at Cormon's studio in Paris against his father's wishes. Here he met van Gogh and Toulouse-Lautrec. His early works are Impressionistic, but in Brittany he was introduced to, and later experimented with, Signac's **Pointillism**. Bernard wanted to find a style of painting in which 'ideas dominate technique', meaning the idea behind a painting is more important than the way it is painted. This style of painting was entirely at odds with that of Cormon and Bernard was expelled from the studio. In 1886 he met Gauguin in Pont-Aven, and developed the style known as **Cloisonism**. They exhibited together at the Café Volpini in 1889. Bernard later quarrelled with Gauguin as he felt Gauguin had stolen his ideas and represented them as his own. He died in Paris on 15 April 1941.

Communication between the two men ended. Gauguin returned to Paris in the December of 1888 and continued to work with the **Symbolists**.

After travelling to Copenhagen to bid his wife and children farewell, Gauguin departed for Tahiti in April 1891. He arrived hoping to find an untouched paradise, free from the corruption of European culture, but **colonial** inroads and the work of **missionaries** had already begun to alter it. Gauguin's health deteriorated. After months of not eating properly he was admitted to hospital. His painting style changed at this time and he produced vast amounts of work. His interest in Tahitian culture led him to compile a book about Tahitian folklore in 1892. The following year he learnt he had inherited a small legacy and returned to France in August 1893.

In 1895, suffering from syphilis (a serious sexually transmitted disease that can lie dormant for many years and then affect the sufferer in different ways), Gauguin returned once more to Tahiti. Here he lived with a young woman called Pahura who bore him a daughter. He named her Aline, in memory of his daughter (with Mette) who had died in 1897. Ill and depressed, he decided to commit suicide after painting his largest picture *Where do we come from? What are we? Where are we going to?*. In January 1898 he took a huge dose of arsenic and prepared to die, but instead of killing him the poison gave him a night of severe and painful vomiting.

In 1901 he moved to the Marquesas islands where another young woman bore him a daughter in 1902. In this year he also incited the natives against colonial government. For this he was accused of libel (a written or printed statement that is damaging to a person or group's reputation) and stirring up **anarchy**, and was sentenced to three months' imprisonment. He appealed against the sentence but died of a stroke in prison on 8 May 1903.

Vincent van Gogh 1853–90

- Born on 30 March 1853 in Groot-Zundert, the Netherlands.
- Died on 29 July 1890 at Auvers-sur-Oise.

Key works

Sunflowers, 1888
Self-portrait with Bandaged Ear, 1889
The Starry Night, 1889
Mountains at Saint-Rémy, July 1889
The Siesta, 1889–90

Vincent van Gogh was born on 30 March 1853 in Groot-Zundert, a village in the Netherlands near the Belgian border. His father Theodorus was a **Calvinist** pastor and his mother was called Anna Cornelia. He was the eldest of six children. In 1864, when van Gogh was eleven, he was sent to a boarding school in Zevenbergen. However, his father's reduced finances meant that he could no longer afford the fees, and van Gogh finished schooling at the age of sixteen and returned to the family home.

In July 1869 van Gogh was taken on by Goupil and Co. and worked in a shop in the Hague selling prints and engravings. At this stage of his life he was a model employee, who enjoyed reading and visiting museums. At the beginning of 1873 van Gogh's younger brother Theo was given a job in the Brussels branch of the company. The brothers began to write to each other. It was a correspondence that lasted seventeen years and records van Gogh's troubled life.

In 1873 van Gogh was transferred to the London branch of Goupil and Co. where he discovered the work of the English artists Constable, Turner and Gainsborough. Their fresh approach to landscape painting impressed him. During the summer of 1873 he fell in love with Ursula Loyer, the nineteen-year-old daughter of a French pastor. Van Gogh proposed marriage and was rejected. He returned home to Holland, sad and dejected. On his return to London with his sister Anna, who was looking for a job as teacher or governess, he sank into a depression that was to remain with him for the rest of his life.

In May 1875 van Gogh was transferred again, this time to Paris. His letters to Theo at this point show an increased interest in religion. He finally left Goupil and Co. and, after a brief stay with his parents, he returned to England in April 1876 to take up a teaching job in Ramsgate. Here he taught French, arithmetic and spelling. He received no pay, only board and lodging.

Self-portrait with Straw Hat, by Vincent van Gogh (1887)
This is one of the many self-portraits painted by van Gogh during his short life.
This image of the artist in his casual clothes and straw hat is painted in the
artist's trademark style with a strong use of colour.

Van Gogh left this job for one in Isleworth on the outskirts of London working at a school run by a Reverend Jones. He became increasingly obsessed with the Bible, especially the New Testament. Van Gogh began to preach in some of the poorest areas in London. When he returned to his family at Christmas 1876 he seemed ill and exhausted. His parents found him work in a bookshop in Dordrecht where he would sit copying passages from the Bible into English, German and French.

His fellow lodger at the corn-chandler's house where he was living in Dordrecht provided a vivid description of the 24-year-old van Gogh. He said, 'He was a singular man with a singular appearance into the bargain. He was well made, and had reddish hair which stood up on end; his face was homely and covered in freckles, but changed and brightened wonderfully when he warmed into enthusiasm, which happened often enough.' His behaviour began to worry his brother. Van Gogh forgot to eat and stayed up throughout the night. He was determined to become a preacher.

To enter the Faculty of Theology in Amsterdam van Gogh had to pass an arduous entrance exam. For fifteen months he studied hard but still failed his exams. He continued his plans for the ministry and started training at a Flemish **Evangelical** school near Brussels. In 1878 he began preaching to the poor miners in Belgium. His religious fanaticism ended in his dismissal from the theological school.

During his time as an Evangelist, van Gogh drew constantly. This helped him to escape from the depression in which he found himself. He decided, at the age of 27, to become an artist. He realized that if he was to express himself properly as an artist, he would need to take steps to develop his technique. Realizing that tuition at a traditional art academy would not suit him he worked with artist friends and was thus essentially self-taught. From 1880 to 1881 he spent six months in Brussels taking lessons in anatomy and **perspective**. The setbacks, poverty and sense of failure that he had endured continued to make him depressed and unwell.

In 1881 he fell in love and proposed marriage to a widow. Her rejection plunged him into another deep depression. He moved to Drenthe, Holland, where he lived and worked in great poverty eventually setting up with a prostitute named Sien, who had modelled for him. This relationship also ended badly.

In February 1886 van Gogh travelled to Paris to stay with Theo. This allowed him to save money and study at the studio of the artist Cormon. Here, for the first time, he saw the work of the Impressionist painters, which he greatly admired.

Colour emerged as an important element in his paintings, having been almost entirely absent before. He also discovered Japanese prints.

In 1887, together with Gauguin and Bernard, he exhibited pictures in a couple of popular restaurants in Paris, but after an argument with one of the managers the exhibition ended. Vincent had been in better spirits at first in Paris but now again became depressed. Fellow artists spoke of his fits of temper, insults, threats and erratic behaviour. His brother Theo, who was finding life almost impossible, described the quality of their life together: 'My home life is unbearable. No one wants to come and see me any more because it always ends in quarrels, and he is so untidy that the room always looks unattractive.'

Van Gogh's Bedroom in Arles, by Vincent van Gogh (1889)
Using clear, bright colour van Gogh created a cheerful picture of his room in Arles in the South of France where he lodged in 1888. He loved the simplicity of the room with its plain wooden floorboards, unadorned window, and simple furnishings of bed, washstand and two rushbottomed chairs.

Van Gogh decided to leave Paris and make a new start, and in February 1888 he left for Arles in the South of France. Here he painted, walked and wrote letters to friends. Soon, however, his mood again became depressive.

In March 1888 Theo managed to exhibit three of van Gogh's pictures. He rented an extra room to store the paintings van Gogh sent to him and sent him an allowance each month.

Gauguin visited van Gogh in October 1888 but the visit ended dramatically two months later when Gauguin, in need of a break from van Gogh, left the house alone. On seeing van Gogh brandishing a razor he felt it safer to lodge for the night in a hotel. Van Gogh went home and cut off his right ear. In the morning he was found in bed covered in blood and taken for dead.

The police were called, and a doctor, and van Gogh was taken to the Hotel-Dieu hospital in Arles. The incident was followed by violent delirium and van Gogh had to be locked up. At this time he painted self-portraits showing his bandaged ear.

■■■ *Wheatfield with Crows*, by Vincent van Gogh (1890)
Painted in the year of his death, this canvas is one of his last works. It is hard not to see the work as prophetic, an intimation of death; the crows fly low over the wheatfield, and the sun is setting above a path that disappears from view.

On 4 January 1889 van Gogh discharged himself and returned to the house where he had been living. A month later he was back in hospital. The townsfolk of Arles believed he could be a danger to them and signed a petition requesting the mayor to remove him. From this time until his death the following year he was barely out of mental asylums. He grew more depressed, more unhopeful of public recognition. In May 1889 he wrote: 'As a painter I shall never amount to anything important now, I am absolutely sure of it.'

In December 1889 he had a violent and terrible attack of madness. As well as being a manic depressive, van Gogh was also probably an epileptic (subject to regular, involuntary and sudden convulsive seizures); he was malnourished and his spirit and body had undergone repeated hardships. He suffered a series of mental breakdowns. At times he accepted his 'madness as a disease like any other' as he put it, and worked enthusiastically on his painting. At other times, however, he found his situation too hard to bear and made repeated suicide attempts.

Van Gogh was invited to exhibit with **Les Vingt** in Brussels and sent in six paintings. He was surprised to read an article by Albert Aurier, an important critic, who was interested in his work. Van Gogh also sold a painting – *The Red Vineyard* – to Anna Boch. Out of the 700 paintings he had produced this was the first sale he had ever made.

By May 1890 van Gogh could no longer bear the asylum he had been a patient in for over a year. He left for Paris where Theo had arranged for him to lodge at Auvers-sur-Oise and to see Dr Gachet. Van Gogh had little faith in Dr Gachet's abilities. He continued to paint but wrote, 'Having returned here, I have found myself feeling much sadder. My life is being attacked at its very root, and the steps I am taking are unsteady.'

On 27 July 1890 van Gogh shot himself. He was found by the Ravoux family, with whom he was lodging, lying in his own blood on his bed. Theo was sent for and arrived the next day. Van Gogh smoked his pipe, spoke his final words to his brother and at 1.30 am on 29 July 1890 died.

Henri Matisse 1869–1954

- Born on 31 December 1869 in Le Cateau-Cambrésis in north-eastern France.
- Died in Nice on 3 November 1954.

Key works

Harmony in Red, 1908
Red Studio, 1911
The Italian Woman (L'Italienne), 1916
Festival of Flowers, Nice, 1923

Henri Emile Benoît Matisse was born on 31 December 1869 in Le Cateau-Cambrésis in north-eastern France. He was the eldest of three children. His father, Emile, was a grain merchant. His mother, Anna, ran part of her husband's shop, selling house paint and advising customers on their colour schemes. Matisse was a docile, obedient child, and his mother was always his greatest supporter.

Matisse was a boarder at the Lycée in St-Quentin before moving to Paris to study law at the age of seventeen. He passed his law exams in 1888 and started work in a lawyer's office. In 1889 he ended up in hospital suffering from appendicitis and spent much of the next year bedridden. His mother encouraged him to paint while he recovered. She herself was an accomplished painter on porcelain and was the person who advised Matisse to listen to his emotions while painting rather than rely completely on the rules of art.

By 1891 Matisse had decided to go to Paris and take up art full-time. His father was disgusted and warned that it would not work out, but Matisse abandoned his law career and began to train as a painter. He enrolled in the Académie Julian and the École des Beaux-Arts, where he studied under Gustave Moreau. His early training was conventional, studying models and copying the **Old Masters** in the Louvre. He spent the summers of 1895–97 painting in Brittany.

In 1898 Matisse married Amélie Parayre, a model he often painted. They visited London, Corsica and Toulouse. To make ends meet, Amélie worked as a hatmaker and then set up a shop of her own while Matisse took a job as a theatrical scene painter. When both Amélie and Matisse suffered illnesses in the early 1900s, they were forced to live with his parents.

Self-portrait, by Henri Matisse (1918)

Matisse shows himself at work, palette and brush in hand, seated in front of the easel, just visible at the lower right of the painting. His reserve and manners, described as those of 'a German professor' can be seen here in the composure of the bespectacled artist, dressed soberly in suit, tie and shirt.

Matisse worried that his father had been right but still continued to paint, inspired by a meeting in 1903 with Paul Signac (an artist interested in **Pointillism**), who had been a co-founder of the Société des Artistes Indépendants, a group of more liberal artists. Matisse enjoyed some success exhibiting with them.

In 1904 he had a solo show at Ambroise Vollard's gallery and spent the summer working with Signac and another Pointillist, Henri-Edmond Cross, in the South of France. Through Signac, Matisse was influenced by the late Seurat's theory of Divisionism (see p 8).

In 1905 Matisse painted with Derain in the coastal town of Collioure in the South of France, something he was to do every summer from then on. It was here that his use of colour changed and led to the famous exhibition at the Paris **Salon d'Automne** in 1905, labelled *fauves* (savage beasts) by the critic Louis Vauxcelles. As the oldest member of the group by some years, Matisse was regarded as their leader.

One of the paintings Matisse exhibited was *Woman with the Hat*, which was bought by Leo Stein, the brother of the wealthy American author and patron Gertrude Stein. The Stein family encouraged other US collectors to buy Matisse's work and also introduced him to Picasso. By 1906 Matisse's reputation was growing and he met the Russian patron Sergei Shchukin, who bought up everything in his studio and, in 1909, commissioned two murals, *Dance* and *Music*, for his house in Moscow.

In 1906 Matisse travelled to Algeria. He was interested in native art and in African sculpture, and the influence of both is evident in Matisse's work. From 1907 he began to travel widely to Italy, Germany, Spain, Russia and Morocco. In 1908 he published *Notes of a Painter* and had his first one-man show in New York, which was not a success. In 1910 he travelled to Munich expressly to see an exhibition of Islamic art.

During World War I (1914–18) Matisse lived in Paris and the South of France, and spent much of his time learning to play the violin. In 1919 he was commissioned to design the sets and costumes for Stravinsky's *Le Chant du Rossignol* (*The Song of the Nightingale*). Official recognition came for him in 1921 when the French government bought one of his paintings and his work began to appear in public collections around the world. He was made a Chevalier of the Legion of Honour in 1925. He continued to travel and in 1930 was commissioned by the Barnes Foundation in Philadelphia to create the *Dance* mural.

The 1930s saw a separation between Matisse and Amélie, although they never divorced. He developed cancer and had an operation in 1941, which left him an invalid. While his wife and daughter were arrested for their involvement in the French Resistance, Matisse continued to work. In 1947 he undertook the commission to decorate the chapel of St Marie du Rosaire at Vence near Nice but was too ill to attend the opening in 1951.

From 1947 Matisse was often bedridden and began to work increasingly with **découpage**, cutting out designs on paper and mounting them on canvas. He died in Nice on 3 November 1954, aged 84.

The Red Room, by Henri Matisse (1908)
This interior with a woman is typical of Matisse. Colour is bold and bright, and there is much decorative treatment of wall and tablecloth to make a surface pattern of colour and shape.

Gustave Moreau 1826–98

- Born on 6 April 1826 in Paris, France.
- Died in Paris on 18 April 1898.

Key works
Oedipus and the Sphinx, 1864
Orpheus, 1865
The Apparition, c. 1874–76
The Sirens, c. 1890

Gustave Moreau was born in Paris on 6 April 1826. His father Louis was an architect to the City of Paris; his mother, Pauline Desmoustiers, was an accomplished musician. Moreau was a delicate child whose parents tended him with great care. Mother and son were devoted, and Moreau lived a sheltered life until his parents reluctantly sent him to board at the Collège Rollin, a high school in Paris. Here he remained for a miserable two years until an unhappy event brought him home. His sister Catherine, a year his junior, died in 1840. In 1841 the grieving family travelled to Italy and it was here that his passion for art thrived. From the age of eight he had enjoyed drawing, but in Italy his father was struck by the sketches Moreau was making in his notebooks. He insisted, however, that Moreau finish his schooling before pursuing his training as an artist.

Portrait of Gustave Moreau, by Edgar Degas (1867)
This image of the artist was painted by Degas who exhibited with the Impressionists. It shows Moreau seated on a chair, and casually turning back, as though caught unexpectedly by the viewer. This romantic historicism was worlds away from the subject of modern life which Degas painted.

At the age of eighteen Moreau joined the École des Beaux-Arts in Paris, training under the artist Picot. Picot's unemotional style did not suit Moreau's character, but influenced him for six years. He left the École des Beaux-Arts in 1850. His work at this time was created in a Romantic style, like that of Delacroix and Théodore Chassériau, who was to become a close friend and mentor.

In 1852 Moreau's parents moved house and Moreau left his apartment to join them. He frequented fashionable cafés and restaurants and visited theatres and salons, welcomed wherever he went.

In 1856 when Moreau was 31, this changed. His friend Chassériau died, and Moreau experienced a profound sadness. He no longer socialized but worked alone in his studio, withdrawing into a solitary existence. He spent the years 1857–59 in Italy where his depression gradually lifted, but he no longer felt the ease and joy of his youth.

Moreau was made a Knight of the Legion of Honour in 1875. In 1888 he became a member of the Académie des Beaux-Arts and then a teacher in 1892. His pupils included Matisse, Rouault and Marquet. He died in Paris at the age of 72 on 18 April 1898. He bequeathed his pictures, studio and house to the nation on condition the house become a museum bearing his name. Since 1903 the Musée Gustave Moreau has attracted many visitors.

Orpheus, by Gustave Moreau (1865)
In a work that takes its theme from ancient Greek myth, Moreau makes a lyrical, dreamlike image of a romantic-looking female figure bearing the head of Orpheus on the lyre that he played.

Odilon Redon 1840–1916

- Born in Bordeaux, France on 20 April 1840.
- Died in Paris, France on 6 July 1916.

Key works

The Grinning Spider, 1881
Ophelia among the Flowers, c. 1905–8
Flower Clouds, c. 1903

Odilon Redon was born in Bordeaux on 20 April 1840 to Bertrand, an adventuring father who profited from the plantations of Louisiana. His mother was a Creole woman of French origin, Marie Guérin, known as Odile, which explains the very rare first name she gave to her son. Redon was a delicate child who was consigned to a nurse and sent to live with an old uncle at Peyrelebade, an estate his father had bought in the Médoc, then a remote region of the French countryside. Here, Redon lived a bleak and lonely life away from his family. He later explained what effect this had on his art: 'It was necessary there to fill one's imagination with the unlikely, for into this exile one had to put something.' His interest in art was fuelled by the year he spent in Paris at the age of seven, where he was taken round museums by an old nursemaid.

Self-portrait, by Odilon Redon (1867)
The melancholy of Redon's character is reflected in this self-portrait of the 27-year-old artist.

Ill health prevented Redon attending school until he was eleven, when he was sent to a boarding school in Bordeaux. In 1855 he began drawing lessons with the artist Stanislas Gorin and tried later to train – without success – as an architect. In 1864 he briefly became a pupil of the academic painter Gérôme at the École des Beaux-Arts in Paris. This was not a good choice of teacher as Gérôme's style was highly detailed, whereas Redon was naturally drawn to the vague and introspective.

Pierre-Cecile Puvis de Chavannes 1824–98

Pierre-Cecile Puvis de Chavannes was born in Lyons in 1824. He studied law at the École Polytechnique in Paris but was forced to leave due to illness. While recovering in 1847 he made his first trip to Italy where he was inspired by the **frescoes** he saw there. A return visit during 1848 made him certain that he wanted to become a painter and once back in Paris he studied under Chassériau, like Moreau. In 1850 *La Pieta*, his first painting, was accepted at the **Salon**. However, the following year his paintings were rejected. This had a lasting effect on Puvis de Chavannes' attitude towards official art organizations, and from this point he worked on his own.

Puvis de Chavannes was best known as a mural painter and for his decoration of buildings such as the Sorbonne and the Panthéon in Paris. In 1873, after serving in the National Guard during the Franco-Prussian War (1870–71), he showed his work at the influential gallery of Paul Durand-Ruel.

In 1877 he was made an Officer of the Legion of Honour, as testament to his services to art. He had a strong influence over younger artists, particularly Gauguin and Signac. In 1897 at the age of 73 he married Princess Cantacuzène, who had been his companion for 40 years. He died on 24 October 1898.

At the age of 24 Redon met Rodolphe Bresdin, an older artist whose visionary and imaginative works excited him. Bresdin was important because he revealed to Redon not only a highly personal kind of art but also a different way of life. Bresdin was a **bohemian**. He had chosen to create his own kind of paintings that might not, and probably would not, attract public attention, fame or financial reward. Redon looked upon Bresdin as a kind of mentor, and Bresdin gave him the confidence to follow his own vision.

In 1870 Redon served as a soldier in the Franco-Prussian War, and after this felt able to embark with confidence on his artistic career. He settled in Paris and worked initially with charcoal. Fantin-Latour taught him **lithography**, that led to his first volume of lithographs *Dans le Rêve (In the Dream)*, which appeared in 1879. His paintings reflect his literary interest in the poetry of Edgar Allen Poe and Stéphane Mallarmé, both frequently described as **Symbolist**.

On 1 May 1880, at the age of 40, Redon married a Creole woman, Camille Falte. In 1881 he had his first one-man exhibition at La Vie Moderne (Modern Life) and in 1884 took part in the **Salon des Indépendants**, which he co-founded, and of which he was president from 1884.

In 1886 he exhibited with the Impressionists. He became relatively well known as his work was shown with **Les Vingt** in Brussels where his strange prints provoked much interest. From 1889 he exhibited regularly at Paul Durand-Ruel's gallery in Paris.

In the early 1880s Redon became friends with Mallarmé and met other Symbolist poets through him. Redon's reputation had been enhanced when the hero of a novel written by J. K. Huysmans in 1884 had collected the drawings of Redon.

Redon suffered a serious illness during 1894–95 and it was after this that a major change in both his personality and artistic style occurred. He became more cheerful and started to use brightly-coloured chalk pastels. In March and April 1894 there was a **retrospective** of his work at Durand-Ruel's gallery and later exhibited in Brussels, Holland and England.

In 1897 he sold the family estate of Peyrelebade after staying there for several months. The following year he showed at the gallery of the dealer Ambroise Vollard, the first of several exhibitions there. In 1899 Vollard published Redon's **lithographs** entitled *The Apocalypse of St John*. The artist Paul Signac organized an exhibition of the work of younger painters in homage to Redon. From this point onwards Redon devoted himself to oil painting and especially to pastels.

Redon was nominated for the Legion of Honour in 1903, and the following year had a special exhibition of over 60 of his works at the **Salon d'Automne**. From 1909 he worked at Bièvres outside Paris. His work was becoming well received outside France; in 1910 his work was shown at Roger Fry's Post-Impressionist exhibition in London. In 1913 over 70 works were shown at the famous Armory Show in New York, where he sold eleven flower paintings for the then very high prices of $300–$400.

In 1911 Redon travelled to Venice, which inspired him to paint a final series of works. He continued working almost to the very end of his life and he died in Paris on 6 July 1916.

■■■ *The Chariot of Apollo*, by Odilon Redon (c. 1905–14)

Redon's work was frequently based on classical subjects. The Roman Sun god Apollo, whose chariot bearing the Sun was daily driven into the sky, provided the inspiration for this work.

Paul Sérusier 1864–1927

- Born in Paris, France on 9 November 1864.
- Died in Morlaix, France on 6 October 1927.

Key works

The Talisman, 1888
Incantation, 1890
Still Life with Violets, 1891

Portrait of Paul Sérusier, by Maurice Denis (1918)
Denis, six years older than Sérusier, has depicted him as a countryman in casual clothes and straw hat. Sérusier, who brought back The Talisman, *was a powerful influence on the group of young artists who became known as the Nabis.*

Paul Sérusier was born on 9 November 1864 in Paris to a wealthy glove and perfume manufacturer of Flemish ancestry. He was a pupil at the Lycée Condorcet in Paris. Uninterested in going into the family business, he persuaded his parents to allow him to study art and entered the Académie Julian in 1885. Here he was very popular among his fellow pupils, an authoritative and intellectual figure with an interest in art and philosophy. In the summer of 1888 he met Paul Gauguin at Pont-Aven in Brittany. He received a lesson in painting that was to lead to the formation of a group of painters known as the **Nabis** (see page 6). Using the lid of a cigar box as a panel to paint on, Gauguin talked Sérusier through the making of a work of art: 'How do you see those trees? They are yellow. Well, put down yellow. And that shadow is rather blue so render it with pure ultramarine. Those red leaves. Use vermilion.'

The result was more **abstract** than Gauguin's own work, and on his return to the Académie Julian Sérusier showed it to his fellow artists, including Bonnard, Vuillard and Denis. He called it *The Talisman*. Sérusier and his friends called themselves Nabis, the Hebrew word for prophet, to signify that they were members of something more far-reaching than a purely visual art movement. Sérusier hoped to create a brotherhood of like-minded artists.

During the summers of 1889 and 1890 Sérusier worked closely with Gauguin, and, after the latter's departure for Tahiti, took over Gauguin's leadership of the artists working in Pont-Aven. During the early 1890s Sérusier exhibited with the Nabis, not only paintings but also theatrical work: designing sets, costumes and programmes.

Sérusier made Brittany his base from around 1890, and his subject matter was often the simple tasks performed by the Breton women: carrying water or laundry, spinning or tending herds of cattle. He also painted murals and decorated the walls of his house with **frescoes**. He developed a colour theory that separated warm from cool tones to avoid their jarring effect when put together, which he disliked in modern painting.

He moved to Châteauneuf-du-Faou, Brittany in 1894 and made that his permanent home until his death in Morlaix aged 63 on 6 October 1927.

The Forgiveness of Our-Lady-of-Doors with Châteauneuf-du-Faou, by Paul Sérusier (c. 1894)
The religious subject matter of this work is typical of that of the Nabis. We see a procession of women in traditional Breton costume headed for the church beyond the gateway in the city wall. The composition is deliberately flattened to create a pattern-like effect.

Georges Seurat 1859–91

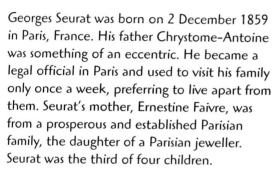

- Born on 2 December 1859 in Paris, France.
- Died on 29 March 1891 in Paris.

Key works
Peasant with Hoe, 1882
Seated Woman, 1883,
A Sunday Afternoon on the Island of
La Grande Jatte, 1884–86
The Circus, 1890–91

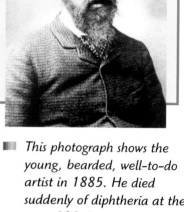

Georges Seurat was born on 2 December 1859 in Paris, France. His father Chrystome-Antoine was something of an eccentric. He became a legal official in Paris and used to visit his family only once a week, preferring to live apart from them. Seurat's mother, Ernestine Faivre, was from a prosperous and established Parisian family, the daughter of a Parisian jeweller. Seurat was the third of four children.

▥ *This photograph shows the young, bearded, well-to-do artist in 1885. He died suddenly of diphtheria at the age of 32, leaving an infant son and mistress. During his brief life he was to exercise a powerful influence on the history of art.*

Seurat spent a great deal of time during his childhood sitting with his mother in the nearby Parc des Buttes-Chaumont. Much of his later art was based on the people he saw at this time. He was introduced to painting at the age of ten by his uncle Paul Hautmonté-Faivre. The secure financial position of his family meant that Seurat had few money worries and, unlike many artists, he did not have to defy his family to train as a painter. He attended an evening drawing course at the Municipal Art School near his home in Paris from 1875 to 1877 and in February 1878 went on to the École des Beaux-Arts.

He undertook his national service at Brest, Brittany from 1879 to 1880 and spent much of his time drawing. On his return to Paris he rented a studio near the family home. Here he set to work on an entirely self-taught programme, beginning by experimenting with conté crayon in a style entirely different from that taught traditionally.

Seurat was influenced by scientists as well as artists. In his book *Modern Chromatics* scientist Ogden Rood described how different colours placed side by side in dots produce the effect of new colours when viewed from a distance. This became the principle underlying Seurat's own theory of Divisionism. In 1886 he met Charles Henry, a young mathematician and art theorist, who believed that all primary colours have a natural, fixed effect emotionally. This greatly interested Seurat. Henry thought that rising lines and bright colour evoked happiness, and descending lines and dark colour provoked sadness.

In 1884 Seurat's *Bathers at Asnières* was rejected by the **Salon**. In response to this he formed a group with Paul Signac, Henri-Edmond Cross and others called the Société des Artistes Indépendants where *Bathers at Asnières* was the centrepiece and a big success.

A Sunday Afternoon on the Island of La Grande Jatte (1884–86) was painted using dots of colour and exhibited in the last Impressionist exhibition in 1886 where it was seen by the critic Félix Fénéon. He wrote about Seurat's work in the new *Vogue* magazine and coined the term Neo-Impressionism as a result.

In 1889 Seurat moved in with his mistress, Madeleine Knobloch, who was to be the model for *Woman Powdering Herself* (1890), and they had a child in February 1890. Seurat had always kept his private life a secret and his friends were surprised to learn of her existence. He only introduced her to his family a couple of days before his death. Seurat died from infectious diphtheria on 29 March 1891. His son died shortly afterwards from the same infection.

■ *A Sunday Afternoon on the Island of La Grande Jatte,* by Georges Seurat (1884-86)
This painting of Parisians enjoying a Sunday afternoon on an island in the river Seine was painted when the artist was in his mid-twenties. The image is created using the application of dots of coloured paint. The technique, known variously as Pointillism, Divisionism and Neo-Impressionism, shows Seurat's interest in the scientific theories of colour, tone and line.

Paul Signac 1863–1935

- Born on 11 November 1863 in Paris, France.
- Died in Paris on 15 August 1935.

Key works
The Dining Room, 1886–87
View of the Port of Marseilles, 1905
Vase of Flowers, 1918

Paul Signac was born on 11 November 1863 in Paris. His father, Paul Victor Jules, a well-to-do shop keeper was 24, his mother Héloïse Anaïs Eugénie Deudon was 20. Signac was a delicate and impressionable child who was interested in art and from a young age visited galleries and exhibitions. At the fourth Impressionist exhibition in 1879 he tried in vain to persuade his family to buy Impressionist paintings. He made a quick copy of a Degas and was told by Gauguin at the entrance to the exhibition: 'One does not make copies here, monsieur.'

Signac on his Sailing Boat, by Theo van Rysselberghe (1886)
Van Rysselberghe has painted the artist Signac engaged in his favourite pastime of sailing. The painter is shown, guy rope in hand, sailor's cap on head, in profile against a white sail.

When Signac was sixteen his father died of tuberculosis. His mother moved with her son and father-in-law to a house in Asnières, a suburb of Paris. Signac began to paint and to sail on the Seine. In 1882 he met Berthe Roblès, a hatmaker and a distant cousin of Pissarro, who he later married. He started to study architecture at the Collège Rollin. His daily route from home to school took him past the art students' quarter and he began dropping in on art dealers and visiting exhibitions. He decided to become a painter and refused to sit his final school exams (although he had excelled academically). He then enrolled at the private art studio of Jean-Baptiste-Emile Bin in 1883.

He began to copy works by Degas and Manet, and to paint in an Impressionist style. However, in June 1884 he saw the work of Georges Seurat at the **Salon des Indépendants**, where two of his own canvases were on show. Seurat had developed a style of painting founded on the process called **Pointillism**. Signac was an enthusiastic follower of Seurat and in 1885 he painted his first Divisionist picture, which he exhibited at the eighth Impressionist exhibition.

From the mid 1880s Signac exhibited regularly at the Salon des Indépendants, and from 1888 at the **Les Vingt** exhibition in Brussels, but he did not have a solo exhibition until 1902. After Seurat's untimely death in 1891 it was Signac who took on the role of chief spokesman and exponent of the theory of Neo-Impressionism. Apart from painting in oils, and from 1896 in watercolours, Signac also wrote. His *From Delacroix to Neo-Impressionism,* published in 1899, is the textbook of the movement.

In 1898 Signac visited London to make what he called 'a pilgrimage to Turner [the artist Joseph Turner]', and from 1910 onwards he was to paint a large number of watercolours. From 1905 until his death in Paris in August 1935 he was president of the Société des Artistes Indépendants.

▌▌ *Women at the Well,* by Paul Signac (1892)
This image of two women drawing water at a well is depicted using the dot method of Pointillism, practiced by Seurat, Signac, van Rysselberghe and others to create an increased sense of luminosity.

Maurice de Vlaminck 1876–1958

- Born in Paris on 4 April 1876.
- Died on 7 October 1958 at Rueil-la-Gadelière.

Key works
Barges, 1908
Red Fields, 1908
Village in the Snow, 1927

Maurice de Vlaminck was born in Paris on 4 April, but passed his childhood at Vésinet where his maternal grandmother lived. Vlaminck was one of five children. Both his parents were musicians and everyone in the family made music – Vlaminck played violin and double bass.

In 1892 he left home and got married in 1894 to Suzanne Berly. He became a champion, professional racing cyclist. An illness prevented him from participating in the Grand Prix in Paris in 1896 and he regretfully had to end his career in sport. He carried out his **military service** in Brittany.

▦ *Self-portrait,* by Maurice de Vlaminck (1911)
The artist shows himself in tie, shirt and suit with bowler hat on head. On the left we can just see the top of the double bass or violin which Vlaminck played, and with which he made his living playing in nightclubs.

To provide for his wife and children Vlaminck again took up the violin, playing in nightclubs and café-concerts. He also wrote articles in **anarchist** publications. Sometimes he painted for pleasure on the island of Chatou, and later wrote that, 'the idea of becoming a painter never occurred to me; to make a career from painting, I would have laughed out loud if someone had suggested such a thing; to be a painter! That wasn't a proper job any more than one could become a professional anarchist, lover, dreamer or boxer.'

However, Vlaminck did end up as a painter, and this was due in great part to his meeting with the artist André Derain in 1900. Derain encouraged him to paint full-time and together they formed the École de Chatou, named after the suburb of Paris where they lived. Vlaminck was largely self-taught.

Vlaminck's first marriage broke up in 1905 and he later married Berthe Combe, to whom he had previously taught music. In 1906, at the **Salon des Indépendants**, he sold a canvas for the first time and earned 100 francs. The art dealer Ambroise Vollard bought all the paintings in his studio and gave him a one-man show in 1907. He also had an invitation from the artist Wassily Kandinsky to exhibit at the second New Artists' Association exhibition in Munich and, in 1912, at Roger Fry's second Post-Impressionism exhibition in London.

From 1908 Vlaminck's work, principally landscape, became more subdued in colour. After World War I he had a second one-man show which allowed him to set up a farm in the countryside near Verneuil-sur-Arve. Like Derain, his reputation deteriorated after he visited Germany during World War II. He was even arrested briefly in 1944 and questioned about his activities.

In 1954 he was invited to exhibit at the **Venice Biennale** and two years later a **retrospective** of his work was shown at a private gallery. He also wrote several novels, memoirs and articles, painted stage scenery and illustrated books. He died on 7 October 1958 at Rueil-la-Gadelière.

Red Trees, by Maurice de Vlaminck (1907)
The deliberate choice of non-naturalistic colour Vlaminck has chosen reflects the fauve use of bright, exaggerated colour. Form is boldly outlined and flattened, and there is an energy and wildness in this canvas which makes it easy to understand why critics called this style of painting fauve or wild.

Édouard Vuillard 1868–1940

- Born in Cuiseaux, France on 11 November 1868.
- Died in La Baule on 21 June 1940.

Key works

Young Girls Walking, c. 1891
Old Woman near a Mantelpiece, c. 1895
In a Room, 1899

Édouard Vuillard was born on 11 November 1868 in Cuiseaux, a small town in the Jura, near the Swiss border where his father, a retired marine infantry captain, served as a tax collector. Vuillard was the youngest of three children. The family moved to Paris when Vuillard was nine, after his father's retirement. His mother made corsets for a living. The workshop in the family home and the simple meals around the circular table were scenes that Vuillard was often later to paint.

Vuillard was educated at the Lycée Condorcet in Paris. The Lycée was located in an area full of publishers, art galleries and theatres, and here Vuillard became familiar with high and low culture. Interestingly, all of Vuillard's future artist associates, the **Nabis**, attended the same school in its fashionable surroundings.

When Vuillard left Condorcet in 1885 he intended to follow a career in the army like other members of his family, but was persuaded by his classmate and artist, Ker-Xavier Roussel, to enrol at free evening classes in drawing. These eventually led to a more serious training as an artist at the École des Beaux-Arts and then the Académie Julian.

Through Maurice Denis, his school friend from the Lycée Condorcet, Vuillard met Bonnard and Sérusier whom he later joined as a member of the Nabis. This group, formed in 1888, focused on the theory of **Symbolism** and was spearheaded by Sérusier, who had been profoundly influenced by Gauguin.

Vuillard's paintings are scenes of domestic life, intimate records of family work and meals, which led to their description as '**Intimist**'. He often photographed family or social gatherings and used these as the basis for later paintings. His paintings of the family home often include his maternal grandmother, who lived with the family until her death in 1893. Vuillard also spent a great deal of time with the art dealers, Jos and Lucy Hessel, who lived quietly in wealthy, but tasteful, surroundings.

Vuillard remained close to his mother until she died in 1928. Vuillard was out of the public eye until 1936 when he exhibited work with other former Nabis. In 1938 there was a **retrospective** of his work in Paris. He never married. He died in La Baule on 21 June 1940.

■■■ *Self-portrait,* by Édouard Vuillard (c. 1912)
This freely painted work where dramatic shadows play across the artist's face shows him turning, as though to look at the viewer, who appears to have interrupted him at his work.

The Next Generation

The influence of the Post-Impressionists on a group of younger artists was immense. Cézanne, Gauguin and van Gogh were all very influential. Van Gogh's belief in the emotional use of colour led directly to the development of the German **Expressionist** artists such as Kandinsky, Nolde and Jawlensky.

Cézanne influenced many of the great artists of the 20th century. His remark about all landscape being made up of the cone, the cylinder and the sphere was the starting point for Picasso and Braque and their investigations into the use of geometric shapes, which led directly to **Cubism**.

Matisse, himself influenced by Cézanne, had a profound effect on the German Expressionist artists, particularly those artists who formed the group known as Die Brücke (The Bridge), such as Kirchner, Schmidt-Rottluff and Pechstein.

Wassily Kandinsky 1866–1944
Born in Moscow, Kandinsky later travelled extensively in Europe. In Paris he became familiar with Post-Impressionism, especially the **Fauve** paintings of Matisse. He was also interested in Seurat's theories about colour, line and **composition**. He developed this interest to its logical conclusion – to the point where the painting was only about colour and shape – an **abstract** work with no immediate reference to the outside world.

Paul Klee 1879–1940
Born in Berne, Switzerland in 1879, Paul Klee went to Germany in 1900 to study art at the Munich Academy. In 1906 he joined Der Blaue Reiter (The Blue Rider), a group of Expressionist artists founded by his friends Kandinsky and Macke. In 1908 he was greatly excited by seeing two exhibitions of van Gogh's work for the first time. After teaching at the Bauhaus school and the Düsseldorf Academy, he was forced to leave Germany in 1933 by the **Nazis**. He returned to Switzerland where he remained until his death in 1940.

Pablo Picasso 1881–1973

Born in Malaga, Picasso left his native Spain for Paris in 1901. He was initially influenced by both van Gogh and Gauguin and their belief in colour as a means of expressing emotion. This led directly to his 'blue' period, the name given to his melancholy scenes of Parisian low-life painted shortly after his arrival in Paris. Cézanne was obviously influential in the beginnings of Cubism. Picasso and Braque experimented with geometric shapes, evolving a style in which they treated their subject matter as a series of faceted shapes.

Georges Braque 1882–1963

Georges Braque was born in May 1882 at Argenteuil, France. Braque studied art in the Louvre and was especially struck by Cézanne's work which he saw in the **Salon d'Automne** in 1904. The impact of the Fauves hit Braque in 1905 when he saw their work at the Salon d'Automne, and he adopted a Fauve style of bright, strong colour. In 1907 Cézanne's interest in geometric shapes influenced Braque and Picasso's Cubist experimentation (1907–14). Braque died in France in 1963.

Still-life with Guitar II, by Georges Braque
Braque's still-life shows the influence of Cézanne's work in the use of geometric forms suggested by Cézanne's remark that all nature is made up of the cone, the cylinder and the sphere.

Timeline

1826 Gustave Moreau born 6 April

1839 Paul Cézanne born on 19 January

1840 Odilon Redon born 20 April

1848 Paul Gauguin born on 7 June

1853 Vincent van Gogh born 30 March

1859 Georges Seurat born 2 December

1863 Paul Signac born 11 November

1864 Paul Sérusier born 9 November

1867 Pierre Bonnard born on 3 October

1868 Édouard Vuillard born 11 November

1869 Henri Matisse born 31 December

1870 Maurice Denis born on 25 November; declaration of Franco-Prussian War

1876 Maurice de Vlaminck born 4 April

1877 Raoul Dufy born on 3 June

1880 André Derain born on 17 June

1882 7th Impressionist exhibition

1884 Establishment of the **Salon des Indépendants** – a jury-free exhibition which offered a forum for experimental artists

1885 Publication of Charles Henry's *Introduction to a Scientific Aesthetic,* which greatly influenced Seurat and Gauguin

1886 Eighth and last Impressionist exhibition where Seurat's *A Sunday Afternoon on the Island of La Grande Jatte* gives rise to the term Neo-Impressionism

1887 Seurat heads a movement termed Divisionism, nicknamed **Pointillism** by the critics

1888 The foundation of the **Nabis**; in October Gauguin joins van Gogh in Arles

1890 Exhibition of Japanese masters in Paris, very influential on Nabis group

1905 October, show of independent artists at the **Salon d'Automne**; term **Fauve** is coined

1910 November, 'Manet and the Post-Impressionists' exhibition opens in London

1912 October, second Post-Impressionist exhibition opens in London

1914 Outbreak of World War I

1918 End of World War I

Glossary

abstract removed from the recognizable. In terms of an art work it describes something not recognizable as an object, landscape or person. A work where colour and shape are more important than what they represent.

anarchist people who believe in destroying the government to attain people's freedom

baccalaureat French equivalent of A levels/high school leaving exam

Baroque dramatic and exaggerated style popular in the 17th century

bohemian unconventional; someone who lives in an informal, flamboyant way

Calvinism religious movement that emphasizes strict church discipline established in the 16th century

Carnegie International/Carnegie Prize annual art exhibition established in 1896 by the Scottish-born American industrialist and philanthropist, Andrew Carnegie

Cloisonism style where thick outlines define areas of colour; influenced by medieval stained glass and enamels

colonial when the government of one country takes over and inhabits other lands. Tahiti was a French colony.

composition arrangement of a painting

Cubism/Cubist style adopted in 1908 by Picasso and Braque to represent objects, people and landscape as constructed by geometrical shapes

découpage making works of art by using shapes cut out from paper

Evangelical Protestant keen to spread the word of God

Expressionism/Expressionist art in which naturalism and traditional ideas are abandoned in favour of an expressive exaggeration and distortion

Fauvism/Fauve comes from *fauve* the French word for savage. Used in 1905 to describe a group of painters using bright, wild colour and style.

fresco painting made directly on a plaster wall

illegitimate describes a child of unmarried parents

Intimists painters of intimate family settings. Developed in the late 19th century by the French painters Pierre Bonnard and Edouard Vuillard.

legitimized when the father and the mother get married their child is made legitimate

Les Vingt society of artists set up in Brussels, Belgium, which supported Neo-Impressionist and Symbolist art in particular

lithograph printing technique invented at the end of the 18th century

military service legal requirement for all men over school leaving age to serve for a year or more in a country's armed services

missionaries evangelical Christians who travel far to spread the word of Christ and convert non-believers

Nabis group of painters who took their name from the Hebrew word for prophet and who often painted religious themes

naturalistic real-looking

Nazis extreme right-wing, anti-Semitic, anti-socialist and anti-communist followers of a political movement led by Adolf Hitler in Germany in the 1930s

Old Masters collective term for work done by famous artists from the past

perspective technique of creating a three-dimensional impression on a two-dimensional surface, based on the observation that parallel lines appear to meet at a vanishing point on the horizon, and that objects become smaller as they rise towards the horizon

Pointillism also known as Divisionism or Neo-impressionism. Paint is applied in points or dots to create a greater luminosity.

primitive art term given by Europeans to non-European art from Africa, South America or Australia

Renaissance rebirth of interest in all things Roman. Began in Italy in 15th century.

retrospective exhibition which shows an artist's work from its beginnings to the most recent

Salon French word for 'drawing room'. It came to refer to a major annual exhibition, in which the members of an art academy showed their latest works.

Salon d'Automne Autumn exhibition

Salon des Indépendants annual exhibition of artists choosing not to exhibit with the official, state exhibition of artists whose work was selected by an official Salon jury

Salon des Refusés exhibition ordered by Emperor Napoleon III and held in Paris in 1863 showing work that had been refused by the official Salon

Surrealists group of writers, artists and film-makers in Paris in the 1920s and 1930s, who took the dreams and the random and chance encounters as the basis for their art and life

Symbolism/Symbolist art movement founded in reaction to Impressionism that aimed to express mystical and spiritual aspects of life in a visual medium. It often explored both religious and erotic images and concepts.

Venice Biennale regular exhibition of art held in Venice, Italy

Resources

List of famous works

Pierre Bonnard (1867–1947)
Dining Room in the Country, 1913, Minneapolis Institute of Arts, USA
The Window, 1925, Tate Modern, London
Dining Room on the Garden, 1934–35, Guggenheim Museum, New York

Paul Cézanne (1839–1906)
Mont Sainte-Victoire, c. 1887
Apples and Oranges, c. 1899, Musée d'Orsay, Paris
Man with Crossed Arms, c. 1899, Guggenheim Museum, New York

Maurice Denis (1870–1943)
Catholic Mystery, 1890
April, 1892, 1892, Kroller-Muller, Otterlo
The Encounter, 1892

André Derain (1880–1954)
Houses of Parliament at Night, 1905–06, Metropolitan Museum of Art, New York
The Pool of London, 1906, Tate Gallery, London
Still life, 1921–22, Art Gallery of New South Wales, Sydney, Australia

Raoul Dufy (1877–1953)
Portrait of Suzanne Dufy, the Artist's Sister, 1904, State Hermitage Museum, Saint Petersburg, Russia
Poppyfield at Lourdes, c. 1908, Art Gallery of New South Wales, Sydney, Australia

Paul Gauguin (1848–1903)
The Vision after the Sermon (Jacob Wrestling with the Angel), 1888, National Gallery, Edinburgh
In the Vanilla Grove, Man and Horse, 1891, Guggenheim Museum, New York
A Farm in Brittany, 1894, Metropolitan Museum of Art, New York

Vincent van Gogh (1853–90)
Sunflowers, 1888, National Gallery, London
Self-portrait with Bandaged Ear, 1889, Courtauld Institute Gallery, London
The Starry Night, 1889, Museum of Modern Art, New York
Mountains at Saint-Rémy, July 1889, Guggenheim Museum, New York
The Siesta, 1889–90, Musée d'Orsay, Paris

Henri Matisse (1869–1954)
Red Studio, 1911, Guggenheim Museum, New York
The Italian Woman (L'Italienne), 1916, Guggenheim Museum, New York
Festival of Flowers, Nice, 1923, Cleveland Museum of Art, USA

Gustave Moreau (1826–98)
Oedipus and the Sphinx, 1864, Musée d'Orsay, Paris
Orpheus, 1865, Musée d'Orsay, Paris
The Apparition, c. 1874–76, Musée Gustave Moreau, Paris
The Sirens, c. 1890 Musée Gustave Moreau, Paris

Odilon Redon (1840–1916)
The Grinning Spider, 1881, Musée d'Orsay, Paris
Flower Clouds, c. 1903, The Art Institute of Chicago, USA
Ophelia among the Flowers, c. 1905–08, National Gallery, London

Paul Sérusier (1864–1927)
The Talisman, 1888, Musée d'Orsay, Paris
Under the Lamp, Finnish National Gallery, Helsinki, Finland
Still Life with Violets, 1891, Norton Simon Museum, Pasadena, California

Georges Seurat (1859–91)
Peasant with Hoe, 1882, Guggenheim Museum, New York
Seated Woman, 1883, Guggenheim Museum, New York
A Sunday Afternoon on the Island of La Grande Jatte, 1884–86,
Art Institute of Chicago, USA
The Circus, 1890–91, Musée d'Orsay, Paris

Paul Signac (1863–1935)
The Dining Room, 1886–7, Kroller-Muller, Otterlo, Holland
Portrait of Félix Fénéon, 1890, Private Collection
The Harbour at Marseilles, 1907, State Hermitage Museum, Saint Petersburg, Russia

Maurice de Vlaminck (1876–1958)
Barges, 1908, Hamburger Kunsthalle, Germany
Red Fields, 1908, Cleveland Museum of Art, USA

Édouard Vuillard (1868–1940)
Young Girls Walking, c. 1891, National Gallery, London
Old Woman near a Mantelpiece, c. 1895, State Hermitage Museum, Saint
Petersburg, Russia
In a Room, 1899, State Hermitage Museum, Saint Petersburg, Russia

Where to see Post-Impressionist artwork

UK
Courtauld Institute Art Gallery, London
www.courtauld.ac.uk

National Gallery, London
www.nationalgallery.org.uk

Europe
Musée d'Orsay, Paris, France
www.musee-orsay.fr

Van Gogh Museum, Amsterdam, Netherlands
www.vangoghmuseum.nl

Statens Museum for Kunst, Copenhagen, Denmark
www.smk.dk

USA
Museum of Modern Art, New York
www.moma.org

Guggenheim Museum, New York
www.guggenheim.org/new_york_index.html

Australia
Art Gallery of New South Wales, Sydney
www.agnsw.com

Internet Disclaimer
All the Internet addresses (URLs) given in this book were valid at the time of going to press. However, due to the dynamic nature of the Internet, some addresses may have changed, or sites may have ceased to exist since publication. While the author and publishers regret any inconvenience this may cause readers, no responsibility for any such changes can be accepted by either the author or the publishers.

Further reading

Most of the biographies listed are written for adults, but feature many reproductions of the artist's work, which will be interesting to young readers.

General

Fauvism, Sarah Whitfield, Thames and Hudson, 1991

Post-Impressionism in the Movements in Modern Art series, Belinda Thomson, Cambridge University Press, 1998

Post-Impressionism in the World of Art series, Bernard Denvir, Thames and Hudson, 1992

The Post-Impressionists, Martha Kapos, Hugh Lauter Levin Associates, 1993

The artists

Bonnard: Colour and Light, Nicholas Watkins, Tate Gallery Publishing, 1998

Cézanne, Nicola Nonhoff in the Art in Focus series, Konemann, 1999

Cézanne, Catherine Dean, Phaidon Press, 1994

Derain, Jane Lee, Phaidon Press, 1990

Gauguin, in the Techniques of the Great Masters series, Linda Bolton, Tiger Books, 1997

Gauguin, Belinda Thomson, Thames and Hudson, 1987

Gauguin, Ingo F. Walther, Taschen, 1994

Van Gogh, Ingo F. Walther, Taschen, 2000

Van Gogh, Andrew Forrest, Hodder and Stoughton, 2002

Vincent van Gogh: The Painter and the Portrait, George T. M. Shackelford, Universe Publishing, 2000

Interpreting Matisse, Elizabeth Cowling, Tate Publishing, 2002

Matisse, Lawrence Gowing, Thames and Hudson, 1979

Matisse Picasso, Anne Baldassari, Elizabeth Cowling, John Elderfield, Tate Gallery Publishing, 2002

Redon, Edda Fonda, Odilon Redon, Firefly Books, 1991

Odilon Redon, Douglas Druick, Thames and Hudson, 1994

Seurat, Sarah Carr-Gomm, Studio Editions Ltd, 1993

Paul Signac, Marina Ferretti Bocquillon et al, Harry N. Abrams, Inc., 2000

Vuillard, Guy Cogeval, Thames and Hudson, 2002

Index

Titles in the *Artists in Profile* series include:

Hardback   0 431 11650 4

Hardback   0 431 11653 9

Hardback   0 431 11642 3

Hardback   0 431 11643 1

Hardback   0 431 11640 7

Hardback   0 431 11651 2

Hardback   0 431 11641 5

Hardback   0 431 11652 0

Find out about the other titles in this series on our website www.heinemann.co.uk/library